October

by the same author

Palm Sunday

Winter Dreams

The Architecture of Holland

Vivaldi, an autobiography

Confessions of Autumn

Avenida Uriburu

October

Matthew Michael Hanner

Chandelier Galaxy Books
Eugene, Oregon

Copywrite © 2015 Matthew Michael Hanner

ISBN: 978-0-9861092-0-1

First edition

cover photograph of the Dordogne at Lalinde by author
author photograph by Toni Hanner

published by

Chandelier Galaxy Books
2015

for Toni

Table of Contents

Casting Off

My Birthday Sonnet   3
After the Parade   4
Four Verses on the Black Keys   5
Snow at Argenteuil   6
No blanket, no hat,   8
Turning the Boats Over Each Fall   10
Sarasota   11
Louie   12
Waiting in Fog   14
Praise God   15
An Afternoon in the Late Eighties   16
Untitled 4/2013   18
Lolita   19
Until It Felt Like Abandonment   20
Here   22

Useful Information

Instructions   25
Explanation   26
Danger   28
Last Thoughts on Climate Change   29
1966   30
Harsh Winds   32
The Moon Again   33
The Finland Station   34
What I Forgot   36
Before Lunch   37
Ornamentation   38
I Found a List of French Colors   39

The Adriatic Concessions

The Dark Before   43
A small block of text   44
Emigration   45
The Vacation Winds Down   46
Conveyance   47
Budapest   48
The Odessa Steppes   49
A City   50
More Geography   51
Afterward   52
Jules   53

Family Gravities

To My Father Dead Now These Thirty Years   57
My Room   58
Christmas Eve   59
Brunch at the Don César   60
Marshall Fields   62
Sanibel   63
He that We Take   64
Paper Boat   65
Wanted   66
Family Gathering   67
Old Boxes   68
Monday Afternoon   69
Square   70
How do you define yourself?   71
Bernard Buffet 1957   72

Further Travel Adventures

Traveling through the Dark   75
The Old Woman in the Yellow House   76
What Night Said   77
Belgium, canned corn,   78
Book Tour   79
Venice   80
Getting from Amsterdam to Paris   82
Beside the Lake   83
The River Vézère   84
Portugal   85
Turkey   86
The Montana Caucus   87
The Upper Peninsula of Michigan   88
Amsterdam   89
Biloxi Morning   90

This Week

Monday   93
Tuesday   94
Wednesday   95
Thursday   96
Friday   97
Saturday   98
Sunday   99

Occasionally August

Considering the End of Summer   103
Port Townsend in Rain   104
Dancers   105
Curious   106
Just Then   107
Thursday   108
Dead at 98º   110

the Gabor sisters take their leave

Blondie   113
Early October   114
Yesterday Afternoon   115
Small Camera   116
My White-Hot Mirror Has Cheek at Night   118
New Book   120
Santorini, Crete or Cornelia   122
Indecision   124
Running in the Dark   125

October

Casting Off

Break the cellophane wrapper, crack the egg, turn the key, unfold the map with your faded pencil notes, strike the face of the cliff against the match, pull the red tab, yank the lanyard of the oily old Evinrude, slide your passport through the wicket where the man in the hat with a shiny black bill waits.

My Birthday Sonnet

A long time ago my parents loved.
Still would have no doubt if death
had not made paper hats of them. Squelched
their marriage which produced only one,
me, now alone but for you, sweet Idaho.
I will tell you things, you who love me despite
the Chinaman with the paper and scissors
and all his glues made from the hooves of sheep.
Businessmen wait in the alcove mincing ham
and oysters for the evening meal, the funeral fête.
My dearest abstract, lithe and aerial, call
for steam, power up the torches and running lights,
the drawbridge is frozen in the raised position.
We are the cowboys you have been waiting for.

After the parade

the elephants would hang out
in the back room at Ruby's.
Mostly they wanted
to get a couple of pitchers down
to take the edge off.
The hot asphalt,
the fuckin' cops
on their motorcycles. Jeeze,
it's nice to sit in the air conditioned dark,
maybe shoot some pool,
couple pails of Fritos,
and while away the rest of the day
till it was time to suit up for the night show.

Four Verses on the Black Keys

A painting almost finished,
rose madder and king's blue.
Boxes of water-stained letters, Georgia clay,
no longer needed. Snow tires for the Mazda.
When I was in bloom, said the old man,
I needed chisels and clamps.
I needed fine strips of bleached linen
to bind those broached by sting and juju.

Of your wistful dawdlings in the old epistles
and souvenirs — leave them in their tru
The sky is saffron at dawn,
close at hand the black bloom of a ranging shot,
later the last train from the Finland Station.
Yeah, I remember it too.
If you need sympathy collect your girlfriends
around an icy pitcher of Mai Tais.

The local fruit jar is out again, parading
freewill on the avenue. He falls over a lot,
his name spelled out in the flashing bulbs.
All the meat in his head is diamonds,
hot and on the hoof.
So much to remember of the future,
when to wait and when to cross,
what to chew and what to swallow.

All that and still no blue to paint the sky.
The earth is molasses and coal.
When I was a boy, when we, when you, you
were only a dark hankering before sunrise,
we fell, judged inferior by ruling gravities.
No one turns to aid the stragglers,
or haul them dark and wet over the gunwales
before pulling away from the wreck.

Snow at Argenteuil

All day more snow has fallen. It turns
the clematis to a cuneiform alphabet.

Say it with a French accent, she prompts,
but still snow is predicted all day. Yesterday,

at the window there was Monet to paint
again The Street at Argenteuil,

the tableaux you sent so many years ago —
images becoming indistinct, color bleeding away.

The woman who posts Fauvist paintings
is in the shadow. Yellow ochre walls lose giddiness.

The figures crossing the road in snow
are now silhouettes gathering winter dark as sun

drops to smolder in the ink and spiders.
The storm has moved the big bitch spider,

who cocooned her prey all Fall on the windowsill,
to wherever her kind goes in snow.

Monet will turn up soon; meanwhile unbuttoning
Gloria's blouse on the mint green carpet,

drinking hard liquor, Peter Dawson scotch
or what have you, realizing winter's arc.

She said after we were past she had wanted
to break through the ice, to hear the sounds

it would make, the intricate disaster occurring,
the calving of another piggish morning to refuse

to birth the sun, any sun, interred, retired
beyond the edge. We know Monet will turn up soon

to paint the homeless here in the church basement.
And here the young dancer in our white town

beaten to death. All day snow falls. Across the planet
Mandela is dead. We're all here in the snow.

Beside the French highway black metal figures
stand marking the sites of each traffic death.

Titanium white, rose madder, burnt sienna.

No blanket, no hat,

It is dawn and everyone is
frightened by the coming dark. All the technocrats
checked their innocence at the door. No hat.

We change planes in Houston, a simple thing.
Returning to a place where I have never been.
No Jacob, no Mr. Eddy, no Mr. Lazlo. No blanket.

The days before you are a cotillion card,
putting her name last is the trick. No baby moons,
no cheap cheroots. Some nebula you remember.

No crucifix. Somewhere glowering at the cross
like old line Marxists with Berthold Brecht
in the back pocket of their black-market Levis.

No squirrel, no wormy chestnuts under the blanket
where thieves break through and steal. If meaning
is important to you, you entered the wrong door.

No lithe and forceful tasteless indiscretion,
with her tiny philanthropies. No hat, but lacey
enough to confuse. Still, he died in a hospital,

but there was no scandal. There was a Cadillac,
there was the endurance of others for a lifetime.
Some nebula you remember, blue

with a streak of yellow, a ghost of those deaths
in white buildings with a sea view. Here the Pacific,
there the Mediterranean or the Sea of Azov, flickering.

The pastel Art Deco curves of the Orange Blossom
Cafeteria, boarded up for six years now,
served dishes for the old, baked chicken, baked cod.

Next week, next year someone will raze it
to build a retirement hotel with a nurse's office,
a card room and central air.

None of those cheap-ass
window air conditioners that drip all the time.
Out where the lighthouse once stood,

wind-ravaged fabric, stacks of gourds,
the remains of a camp, left quickly.
The trick is vanishing while the iron is hot.

This is human laziness, some nebula,
down in the extravagant dirt we forge tomorrow.
We'll wait for you.

Sticky Priscilla and the boys from the Laundromat
are waiting for the number 52. It's late again.
Down in the dirt the roots of the sea are creeping close.

Turning the Boats Over Each Fall

It's the last year I'm going to do this, she says.
We could finish tonight, he thinks,
but she's had it. He could bitch,
but he's been dragging for the last half hour.

They stand behind the boat house,
the oars hung in the rafters, thirty-four row boats
hauled up, turned over on sleepers in the parking lot,
homes for small animals over the winter.

Inside he pours her coffee from a metal thermos.
It's a little too cool to be called hot,
but they drink it looking out at the lake
where the cold wind ripples the dark surface.

Sarasota

We gathered before the makeshift oil drum altar, faces painted indigo, necklaces of wishbones and purple coquinas. It's a little mystic, she said, you know, spiritual. Be that as it may, I was going to tell you about this girl in the navy blue shirtwaist.

We were mostly back. Ready to swing some cats to find the outer edges of this small universe: the old television, the broken couch, a collection of seashells found on Sanibel, back before the bridge to the mainland was built. In Sarasota

we drank water from a 55-gallon plastic drum fed by downspouts. It had a brackish hint from what the wind brought in. There was fire out in the Glades. He's yelling for her to either pack the suitcase and go, or put it back under the bed and stop all this fucking around. With a southern wind

we could smell the smoke those deep warm nights when we sat out on the six by nine whitewashed slab some fool had called a patio. This was in the days when everyone smoked Winstons or Pall Malls, vacationed in the Wisconsin Dells. The wind was from the north then. Her salty figurehead, muff and tangerine dumplings, the fires were close to home. Some nights

we could see the glow on the horizon. The way she smelled when she walked by close. If it was spiritual that was OK, but it was all about picking out her scent from the winds swirling about. It's only the whoop-ass, the silvery ones, that leave the scars and tribal tattoos behind the ear. Souvenirs as the romantics say. Outside the wind wrapped the navy blue shirtwaist against her body.

Louie

He arcs a scrubby red apple to the pen's lone sow.
Her relish at this petite kindness, a gambit repaid,
that is my father as a boy.

There are some girls somewhere, say Canada,
who check each usage of pernicious and dandelion.

What I'm trying to say is someone is always watching,
a small blond with a harelip,
an old codger with a Dutch boathook and a loopy grin.
This is Highway 30, almost Colorado
or some other vast America.

He would record our parade on his ancient Graflex.
My black and white childhood. On white sleeves
hash marks indicating not rank, but patience,

the ability to endure. My father is nine years old.
Time to shoot Louie, says some donkey,
some hand job from any street corner.
I'm getting soft in my dotage. Too ready to forgive.
So we shoot the pig again and again
in the muddy field with a handgun.
The report bounces back
from pale ocher bluffs along the Mississippi.

Here is a picture from the black album.
It's any photo you can conjure up.
The rank excess of a rococo façade in far Bavaria,
your sister, R, with a failing liver
waiting for her god outside Canterbury Cathedral.

These small pawns bob to the surface,
remnants of the carcass below.
So there are two boxes of ashes,
two dogs creeping onto the back porch,
hoping for supper. You follow?

I loved my father. For a theist not a bad sort,
witty, without the twenty pounds
of sententious rhetoric one might expect,
but here is the darkness again
waking, neon letters in the black telling me,
not yet morning.

This is Kansas, where they,
my acrobats, my clockmakers,
once awaited their next brief trapeze.
If caught with courage then another short arc,
another tiny platform, the head of a pin.
What glamour then? What heart? What path?

Waiting in Fog

Beneath the billboard advertising Midway Statuary
on Airport Road, the bliss of her touch. I'm saying,
Hello, as I always try to do in a friendly way

to strangers. This is who we are, a small boat,
a handful too many passengers and more
bobbing to the surface to tip their hats.

I'll have the white meat, I say to the snood, slapping
my hand off camera to show I was well brought up;
carried here in a bassinette of palm fronds.

I don't think about Chesterfield cigarettes
as much I used to. They exist now only as braggarts
in my sub-conscious, separating the rage from sanity.

On the right you can wait in line to buy the latest
black knob. Turn left, here's a crow holding a scented
buff calling card with your name spelled out.

You won the lottery, some Shasta daisies
in a cut-glass vase, a bowl of hemlock plus
a six hundred pound statue of Ganesh, painted pink.

That was the end, but I thought you might like
me to thank you for listening. Much obliged.
If you're out at night wear bright colors.

Praise god,

the cherries are good again this year.
The boys outside are still looking
for some pussy and a wink.
They murmur as the innocent
chalk down the names of the tardy,
pose for photographs of the disappeared.

Crumpled, but still able to cough up a smile,
our loopy grins that belie the coal and gristle.
I spit every pit in hopes it will become a tree
knowing it won't. Still

the options all lead to the same end.
Still she's the only one to blame,
our founder. Opening and closing,
calling and sending away,
offering a bit of Stilton on toast while
touching the throat.
This grandeur, the ego,
the velvet cunt of god,
spewing us higgledy-piggledy into the stars.

An Afternoon in the Late Eighties

Do you remember Olivia
or a woman like her
saying these three words:
raw, ground, round;
separating egg yokes into clear glass bowls
on the white enamel table?

In twenty years she'll sell the house
to a developer who will tell her
he loves the house. No lie,
but he'll be on the horn
to the knackers the same day he signs.
People in the eighties were special.
They believed everything they could.

We finished all the burgundy, said David,
eyeing the Mateus. The old dog dies,
someone backs over the kitten.
Minnie breaks her hip before leaving.

This was now the nineties.
History was sleeping in the side yard.
It had fleas and a goiter the vet said.
He wanted to keep his eye on it with tests
every couple of weeks for $134 per.
There's a kid at the Burger King
passing around a chafing dish of Vienna sausages —
the kind mother serves at parties
to the other old gals widowing in St Pete —
that's how they say it in Pinellas County so as not
to be confused with that place in Russia.

2001. Up at the end of the lake is a lodge
and some cabins. Drive up,
it's the future anyway
when nothing works any more.
She'll be washing down the white table.
Lifting heavy stacks of plates to pine shelves.
I've already said, *I'm sorry,*
but I'm not apologizing, just expressing regret.
Two concepts easily misconstrued.

Untitled 4/2013

Luminous zealots line the approaches to the whisper,
the dove cote and a generous toke to make you docile.
My sweet Buster and confidant: Dawn is yet to break.
Slant light creeps in. *Light*, he said, *does not creep*.
Studying again the map of the Luxembourg Gardens;
walk the panhandle and sit by the observatory fountain.
Watching tourists and lovers hoisting their skirts. Blue
lights line the runway. Come home, the words oscillate,

gasp. Dance is limited by having two feet. If you gnu
what I do, the zoo keeper said, winking at the sparrow.
The number scrawled on the matchbook is a kin of Eve,
some bliss supposed, a dollop of heroics and high tone
before the hoisting, the loud scudding of the clouds.
Here: a silver spoon to use discretely when pouring
sweet curses into the ear. On the screened porch
the kid with the trumpet is untasted, ticking like a bomb.

Old men passing the blue hours, wondering how many
more moons through the high windows, everywhere
specious data, untested at these high latitudes,
but worth a first date smeared with starlight. A
distended, summer sun austere harangues all with hot
platitudes, up to their apps in bubble wrap. Our luscious
rot is too refined. Each willow by the brook is a tender
theatrical device, whipped and unworthy, yet back to
breathe and walk with bump and swagger.

Lolita

Of the fourteen-year old
he left behind in the old Airstream
parked behind the big house,
no one is sure who has custody.

You could be in bad trouble.
What if she's been molested?
He said he was from Iceland.
He said she was his daughter.

But now he is in the Ukraine,
fighting with the partisans
or maybe it's Turkmenistan.
That part of the world,
like his note, is a little vague.
Did I mention there is also a goat?

Until It Felt Like Abandonment
for Keli and Sherry

The ink is quite faded. What solace that Jackie Onassis
might have worn one like it, a little of the potency,

poignancy all seek. Solace, a sip of communion,
a nice Pinot to welcome our comrades, fellow travelers.

We wait, Olympian, but for swollen feet, bad breath
and worries about the passports. What solace?

Avoid the Holiday Inn at the airport in Toulouse,
ask for beer from the girl you loved at seventeen.

Do you think we six, marvels of our age, are flawless?
Curiosities, bone china, whispers beyond paper walls?

My suggestion, keep playing around. Condensed down,
play again without questioning what's missing.

What solace? The blood splattered dress left until later.
Take something ordinary: a day of shared burdens.

Consider: Spring in a white chamois with pearl buttons?
A glove on the stair? The Balkans cleared their throats.

On the day her first husband died of some innocent
denial, of someone in the back seat hoping for sunrise;

Riga unbuttoned to her waist. A cold and Baltic day.
We write about absence, kissing nipples, remembering.

Walking out on the breakwater as far as the pylon
where the blue sea lamp burns. Grip tragedy by its neck,

a chicken to have its neck rung for dinner.
Sentences start with "What solace?" loiter.

Have we not beat upon each other enough? What blossom is unburst? Dying fits late hours.

Some cheap Indiana. *No reservations*, says our Queen untying your motley irks and ills.

All I know is the cadaver looks the same, windswept, without a spinnaker. And yes, I'm asking you to lie.

Here

We begin on our feet, lured and grafted by our terroir,
the boat house that bore us buoyant, we,
this bag of spoke shaves, is but wicker and tarnish.

Again the silver salesmen and their fried cheeses
lead us spore and freeway. *Don't get your hopes up*,
says the lady with the stop watch.

We awoke full grown on this hurtling and gorgeous
globe.
Stop telling me the rules, I have eaten my limit,
sucked the fresh from each slim bone.

Here is the descendent, the mother, the father,
if you have siblings, kiss their cheeks.
They are all you've got for teachers, fellow travelers.

Useful
Information

Knowing where to stand, pointing, more facts about pigs, how to boil water, how to wait. Also we speak of clams, lollygagging, tearing out the sod with a mattock. You get the picture. Enough debris to last a lifetime.

Instructions

Step One:
Obtain the following materials: Twenty-two best-quality ostrich feathers, paper towel, one pint can industrial strength mucilage, Mr. Sticky or approved equal. Tools required: Staple gun, travel size can of Barbasol, a straight razor.

Step two:
Shave the attachment areas, rinse and pat dry.

Step three:
Trim feathers to equal lengths and divide into two equal groups.

Step four:
While holding one group of feathers spread them like a hand of cards and gripping firmly to maintain this shape, dip the fat end into the mucilage and apply. Reinforce bond with staples. Wait 20 minutes before allowing pig to fly.

Explanation

Because I had waited for the others to catch up.

Because this was unusual, they hesitated,
keeping their boats several hundred yards
from the beach until after sunset.

Because we had no shelter.

Because all the photographs were burnt in the fire.
Because, because, because where do I begin to continue?

Because it was the end of that Adriatic summer
when the barren islands along the coast were strung out
like that dusty necklace of shark's teeth
tucked between rebuilt sonars and directional finders
in the window of Rolo's Marine.

Because the roaches ran when the lights came on again.

Because we only had batteries
for the portable radio or the emergency lamp, not both.

Because if we stop to rest, all the people waiting
to be born will be getting obstreperous and moody.

Because Reverend Ted passed it daily heading up the
hill to the rectory of St. Bartholomew's.

Because he invariably gnawed at a root beer taffy
from the shop on Front Street
in whose window an ancient machine labored,
pulled at the gobs of candy like a miniature
of the pump jacks sucking Oklahoma from Oklahoma.

Because Oklahoma was where Ted's mother
had once said their people —
actually, she had said, *Your people,* —
came from.

Because now, near the end, everything winds down
to a level of background radiation
that some of us, even Ted, have learned to tolerate.

Danger

Step Back from the Door, said the first.
I put on a shirt and later kissed the dog.
Brush your Teeth, said the second sign.
We went out to the bluff
and drank too many bottles of Orvieto,
plus a little Valpolicella.
Be of Good Cheer, said the third sign.
We walked back to the church hoping
the boys had not tagged anything
that would be difficult to clean.
The building maintenance fund was on empty.
This could get ugly, thought Ted.

Last Thoughts on Climate Change

A Tiffany egg or a Rauschenberg sheep
is art and not

this bad news.
We waited too long,
out on a limb and no exit.
I really am sorry about this.
It's the point when even a fool can see
too much water is coming over the gunwales.
We bail with Mikasa tea cups.
It is such a lovely planet
we've been lucky enough to live on it for a while.
In these last years
let's be as kind to each other as we can.

1966

I walked into a vestibule of the building,
not understanding about doors yet...
how they move, when they move.

Inside the patient rows of brass mailboxes waiting
Hello, he said extending autumn.
The eye of needle, the Sublime Porte.

Later in Lincoln Park origins,
Hello, I said, darkly Appalachian, acute.
Each path and vector knows my name.

Break out the Peter Dawson,
cut loose the rafts we have towed astern.
Hello, I keep saying until I get it once and always true.

We stand there beside the mailboxes, youths.
Our toes grip the edge of the ten miter board.
We shake hands, kiss on the mouth, *Hello, Hello*.

My wife marvels at computers, all the switches marked:
zero, one. All the doors locked and unlocked
Hello diffuses decorum, unsheathes the meat.

Choristers, sing me the song,
tell again of each blow to shape the steel.
Now there is the remainder of my life.

We tilt our heads and tap our noses passing.
One, *Hello*, paints objects red or blue,
each a letter to a maiden aunt —
now different from what could have been.
The path began as we stamp snow from our shoes.
Jumping rock to rock to avoid moss, avoid the eulogy.
He reached in to hand me the rest of my life.

This is how love starts and stops,
mistake the teacher for the taught.
Each exquisite hot meat is the constitution we bear.
People pass around us, walk the effigies
of dogs to take the air in Lincoln Park.
or they twist their combinations,
hoping for love letters to mitigate the world.

This is my steel,
climbing on the slender apparatus
the engineers have wrought for us —
even now to speak of the cancer is repellent.

Humans, cancers and viruses
possess the inability to say,
No, Thank you. I've had enough.
Day glow wrist bands and party hats.
This is how we dance the dances of the old.
We are a dense group
like stars before collapsing in on themselves.

The begging, the hope, the propitiation for our sins,
our considerable sins — if these are sins.
There must be a god to tell us,
show us our foibles laid out
like hungry babes in a nursery.
The attendants passing up and down the aisles
like nurses or others with supposed fiduciary interests.

Harsh winds

buffer each corner and edge.
Sun flairs faces of cyclists passing.
Bête noire,
some chatty bit of charcoal
our inalienable hallowed,
our inalienable whitewashed.

Tomorrow is bad weather,
insolent days,
wacky, prodigious things
we wrestle them like oiled Turks.

It's mistaken identity.
Blame the moon if you have a mind.
But here at the broom factory
everyone is treated like family.
Take the last bus.
Get off at the end of the line.

The Moon Again

There is the moon again,
Hanging out with the boys by the underpass,
passing a bottle behind the blackberries.
There is the moon again,
coming in my window,
reminding me of blanched faces.
Gone now.
Ash and gaudy,
slim as a pike.
Old moon
coming in my window.
Here are the seas again
swinging round on their leash.
Shine on blue girl, whispers, lollygagging,
roll out the tall tales,
the incantations, colorless in brighter light.

The Finland Station

Sometimes at night returning via the back lane,
I see her walking the dog. It strains at the tether.
As she walks the promontory of night seems to wrap
her and her dog in my headlamps. He leads her,
swaggers his small leashed planet.
Chanterelles caught deep in the November wood,
a pile of dung, oiled leather — you sort the dark,
lumbering vapors that hypnotize us, authorize
on which side of the lock one stands.
Food will tell you the whys. The dog waits
in the twilight of old and curtained rooms. —
safe as Lenin in his sealed train. Beyond the door
she says it's all mildew and sooner or later
you'll find rough edges and tomahawks outside.

This is your leash, she says in the hot, circular mornings.
These will be your walls today and the ceiling above,
> *that is your sky.*

The curtains are never pulled back. In summer
the door is never ajar to pick the cool airs after supper.
The surveillance photographs will back me up.
See here? And there?
That's the plastic sheeting she stapled in the windows.
How long could the dog — we'll call him Ansel —
live before the air grew thin?
The mind is racked with such thoughts.

Pig's knuckles, joule bacon, trotters and grits and beans
cooked almost to a paste like they do in the south.
I only know she's gone when her car is gone.

She works at the Discount Mall out by the 405.
I saw her there once without the dog, who was probably
breathing its last in the darkened rooms.
Walking by her door I never hear a television or a radio.
Although once when her car was gone
I heard her dog singing Cole Porter's
All Through the Night in a lovely tenor voice.

What I Forgot

I forgot:
How to with the big Stilson under the front seat.
I forgot the penchant for enormity,
for looking beyond the breadbox,
checking the larder for whatever it was.
I have lost the bridle,
all the teeth woven into the necklace.
I have forgotten the name you pinned to my chest.
The scar remains though.
The incursion, the incision,
I had forgotten too.
I forgotten the coming and going,
but not the being and waiting.
I remember where the anger lurks,
sturdy and dependable.

Before Lunch

A man sitting at a table
opening a clam
with an oyster knife,
only it wasn't called an oyster knife,
it had another name here.

My baby tells me the plum
she threw out to the crows
was the sacred heart of Jesus.

Ornamentation

I diminish. Loitering about this life, this warthog on ice,
my sweet parody, I am warned about the loss of muscle
mass. My wife worries at the stone terrace I have
undertaken, hauling sand and stone. I do diminish. I tell
her I'm fine and I hope it is true. Tearing out the sod
with a mattock. The cant of my lingo laboring as always
to please, to pick the lock and let the crazies in, their
ineffectual magic stillborn. Under the glossy drone of
another American day the interminable momentum.
Under the neon red preposterous sign the old men
expect CNN to deal the answers out. Jokers face down. I
diminish, but enough about me.

Did you grow up as you hoped?
Did she love you back?
Did you earn every coin in your purse?
Ever figure you'd be sleeping under the bridge, still?

Sometimes I watch Max work, How does his lumbering
carcasses house what little gaudy he can boast. I'm busy
moving and diminishing, wonder how many more years
before I look at stairs with dread, like sitting up all night
in coach. Then I am buying iron, DC motors, studying
how to build an elevator by midday. It will be grand my
old age, dotage, the vestibule of an ancient hotel. The
elevator looks risky, so we take the stairs. There'll be
enough debris to last a life time. The sound of colors
passing overhead is only the breaking up of the smaller
stars.

I Found a List of French Colors

Another year begins today
to listen to the mostly mediocre bums
who sell me politics.
What a coincidence,
the fools have found their way home again.
Approximately starved on this muck
I found a list of French colors.
I learned ten ways to roast a chicken.
And today,
the last day of August,
cars with football banners pierce the town,
approximately August,
spacious and filthy, the grit of our pastime.
Across the road the old man's house stands vacant,
not empty, vacant.
Someday his heirs
will make up their minds.
The zinnias stand,
frozen fireworks in morning's cant light.
More asters will be blooming,
passing time here in the lowlands.
How are things in your town?
All sweet grass and ripe melons?
Someone is always selling scent to mask the latest fad.
I will translate approximately a list of French colors,
not lilac,
I am thinking oxblood
or as they say in France, *sang de bouef*.

The Adriatic Concessions

You know the ship is passing close in shore. You can hear the voices of the deck hands, the Greek verbs rising and falling in the fog. You can't see the light burning in the harbor master's shed, but then the Greek can't either. Tomorrow the sea will be empty and the woman from the north gone.

The Dark Before

The man in the white uniform is waiting.
His silver punch will validate your ticket.
He points to the X where you are to stand.

Another morning to watch rain reconstruct
each convoluted life. So simple really,
just keep breathing, blinking at the brightness.

The fourth cataract is the bitch.
All the boats pulled up to scout the rapids.
I'm voting for the one with the Radar Range.

I speak English with a German accent.
The women in black wait. Silence is their rage.
We inadvertently gave them back their birthrights.

So this is how it usually goes. We lie to them
and they lie to us — we are small people
with ample egos. I felt like, yes, drowning.

I said, *You don't know me*. Inside the water
rose as I fumbled for keys, hand on a brass knob,
the boats adrift, the gulls drunk on blood.

Speak in tongues. Don't say, *You are drowning*.
I want new information, not old news.
No one is singing; no one knows the lyrics.

Outside the morning is paved with leaves.
Dazzling colors paper over the latter days
as we grind down to the dark before Christmas.

small block of text

When I last walked past the apartment building on Viale Trastevere there were no names that I knew on its polished brass plaque. But I remember the worn pitted marble sill of the kitchen window of Stefano's apartment where I would lean to engage the whole panorama of Molly's kitchen. Molly illuminated, Vermeered by window light only. The narrow stove, the sulphurous scent of the match, Stefano out somewhere on the balconies watering his nasturtiums. The tang of the onion, the hot pan, the olive oil, the capers and garlic, the chalk green walls and outside the sweep of Gianicolo Hill rising in a hundred shattered greens, carved where Mussolini's half-finished monumental stair marches up the hill. All that wine.

Emigration

> Just open your feral thieving mortal heart to the stars.
> Dean Young

Lying there in the gray hours,
the sheets smelling vaguely of soap, someone
is speaking of Trieste, of a thin new moon
hung out over the Adriatic.

The stars are thieves, Just and Honorable,
crucified, on their many crosses, mortal.
Someone was kissing
while we were away at this or that small war.
No fresh-squeezed juice on the marble counter.
No white-liveried servants to brush away the crumbs.

You know when I speak of other women
it is always your tongue I touch.
Soon south and further
south we will cross Brindisi to Corfu.

Each a door with a different adamant vista to ogle.
Earth's dark goings and arcs among the feral stars.

In the narthex of a white-washed church
a hunk of hide — the heart gone missing.
The rest we left by the road,
under a bridge with the homeless,
where the rich admire each other's cufflinks.

Deep in the hot and spacious heart, the incense is field
stubble, hot tar and smoke from the fires to the south.
The locals are preparing for football, the end of the
world, new duds from the local toggery.
Finally, passports stamped in red.
At Customs, your cases will all bear the white chalk
mark
of the Interior Minister's inspectors. Lucky you.

The Vacation Winds Down

Ted was a side of beef slumped in any director's chair
strewn before any seaside café you'd care to name.

One boat a week up the coast.
You don't know if she still loves him or he her.

Waiting in Madam Cleo's guesthouse three more days
because of the money. There was a boat to Corfu,

but again this late in the year deck class was dicey.
All those years he had remembered: clapper and bell.

The alphabet is all wrong, suffocating. The chalk scrawl
on the harbor master's shed looked like Greek,

perhaps it was. The date, next to the word
she had said meant Venice, was still Sunday.

The waiter placed two more drinks on the table,
two more small white plates of olives.

Conveyance

There are no assigned seats in the vast,
the homely line for dental care

or a plate of finger sandwiches. Throw back
the eau de cologne, but decide before

you arrive at the dividing platform:
the catfish fried in corn meal

or Alexander's on Andrassy for coffee
and a goggle at its ornate ceiling.

Choices come quickly, catch the baby
or don't. Want chilies with the fish?

At the house on the D703, men
in orange measure the road;

they stand close as matadors.
My shutters are cornflower blue,

but so were the shutters
of every house in the village.

In Budapest remember this name:
Deák Ferenc tér, the park

where three metro lines
cross in the dark. Deep

escalators haul men and women
to the surface like coal.

Budapest

Years, waiting for the number 2 tram,
waiting to buy some pig ears and a goose
at the Central Market.

You have forgotten what little Turkish you knew.
Armloads of white bedding,
women carrying bundles of clouds.

The revelation was nylon.
Americans gone wild. Beefy bruisers
with cab driver boyfriends. Your path is upward

as long as the rest are falling.
So then the revolution is trusting man. Believing
these door knobs are still the jack of diamonds.

You're the blond girl with crooked teeth.
Sometimes he waits in the darkened car
until the proper time to arrive.

You're wearing the dress that shimmers
with all the blues of a peacock. He'll turn to you,
and begin slowly with the uppermost button.

The Odessa Steps

Four AM and red and blue lights flash on the avenue.
Well, I couldn't sleep anyway so I watch the cops
do their cop dance for a while. Later lemons,
samovars, loud clocks, and blue pansies
in stripes through the garden. The old Finn leans
in, plants woolen elbows on my drawing board.
Dawn is coming earlier now as spring unreels
another year. Each year's daffodils and rain
adjust to the earlier comings, the foolish new calendar.
Here is another unwanted prodigal now
with the latest brassy horn or gold tooth to sell.
His face is patches of missed whiskers. He brushes
away the spilt tobacco of a man living alone.
Listens to the BBC at 5AM.
Of course the rest of world knows the answer.
It's Putin in the Crimea.
There is always the Black Sea Fleet to remember.
The baby carriage on the stairs. Bump, bump, bump.

A City

A collection of gravities, an incident
repeated with strangers, the wanderlust
of bricks, riverboat gamblers and the poor —
walking on their knees to impress
with their diligence and deference
the lords of each new shit hole
to own the name of village or burg.

We are a communal species.
Slopping up fine dining at the Imax;
building parks with needles, oaks and foxglove.
We lure the desperate
to do the laundry, lay the rails.
Gold shows the respect one holds
papering the church domes with thin
sheets of gold, ingots are at the bank.

More Geography

The price of fire is going up, but the man in the toll
booth will still cut your silhouette in black paper
for a few euros.

And, yes, I knew them all, the woman with the crooked
walk, loping up the street, the near-miss at the rural
airport, nights thinking about rowing out into the lake.
Easy,

that is to say the thinking, the deft placement of the
hand is a matter of conscience, remembering the
gestation period of memory, and the news again of riots
in France — this can continue late into the temperament
of evening.

Gorgeous and sensitive
are lumped up against each other.
Beasts exhausted from the rut,
privy to the small bleedings.
The barber is closed Monday;
hardly fretful news on the face of it.

The rest of them I've never met.
And probably won't. We breed too fast
for a race so clumsy with the truth.

The rib shack down the road is boarded up
and up for sale. The price of fire going down,
what with the sinister sound of continuing breakage,
the windows rattling in the wind.

The filaments in our garments cool. Each intricate loss
is a white cotton Sunday dress with hem appliquéd
with hand lace work. On the bodice a dainty tea stain
in the shape of an unknown, possibly Asian,
honey-colored country.

Afterward

In the sink her socks and smalls soaked,
a warm glass of Orvieto balanced above the bowl.
In the upper hall paper streamers still hang. Lemons,
cut with blunt scissors from coarse yellow paper,
are taped to the windows
of the dead woman's classroom.

The physician heats her lance in the blue alcohol flame.
Memory is still the thief we fear.
Walking up the cobbled street from the bus station
she hears the piano before turning the corner
to the old hotel, remembers
this was the beginning again
just before everything starts to come apart.

Jules

Before I left
I meant to take the marker from his grave
but the intention was lost in the final hectic days,
the desperate
hanging from the undercarriage
of the last departing plane.

Perhaps no one will recognize
the round disk of babinga
for what it is.
My carving of the English sunrise motif
is without words,
a safe enough disguise
if no one goes digging.

Family Gravities

In which the expected contestants bite and whinny. There is gravy, skim milk, fresh tomatoes, coconut palms and ruined asphalt. We see the sun careening into rooms, find crystalized sultanas, salted walnuts and exotic birds. Each day verticality seems more abstract.

To My Father Dead Now These Thirty Years

Mostly I want to say, *Thank you.*
You are the birch peg my hat hangs on.
You are the wall that holds the peg.
Still, you are dead and not at home
to pay my postage due.

Hello again. Forgive me for not writing,
but you're still dead, not taking calls.
I wanted to tell you everything that happened.
Explain how all that Jesus stuff never flew with me.
But if you were here today,
come down from that pearly nowhere,
still I could not do it.
Could not disappoint you.
All those endless letters I wrote. *It's sunny today.*
I'd say or, *It rains.*

Anyway because today you are only ash,
a misdemeanor, a butterfly on the grill,
I can say atheist.
There is no god to put up pickles for.
Zilch. It's cold out there.
And the real reason the first marriage failed
was not that we grew apart
it's that your god
invented the seething gravity of women
and I am but a moth.
Existence then is the core of all loss.

Of course you are still dead, still the peg,
and I am still your hat.

Michael
3 February, 2013

My Room

My room was the room of my grandmother until she broke her hip and went the way of her mother before her. 1954, the land crabs clatter over the concrete outside my window. My father steps again and again on the memory of the same scorpion.

Three showers a day to buffer the heat, our clothes never dry since April. A Grumman Albatross rumbles overhead to land in the bay out beyond the grove of coconut palms.

For a special Sunday night we drive to Biscayne Key to eat in a restaurant with air conditioning; but usually for our Sunday dinner we walk up to Carl's, to sit on the screened porch under the black ceiling fans that crank the cigarette smoke and hot odors of frying chicken around and around in an imagination of an offshore breeze, a zephyr from Cuba where Batista still rules, counting out turnips for the peasants.

Christmas Eve

We are the last dancers on the floor
when the hall closes at four.
The market noise almost drowns the Canaro *milongas*.
We laugh gliding over missteps in my sloppy lead.
Today the dance is pivots and *trespies*.
We hold this flame to the face of Winter's geometry.

She used to take the train north
and stay in the Mallory Hotel in Portland.
She would eat a secluded dinner in the dining room.
Paired white columns with gold painted capitols
below a thick white cornice,
chandeliers and indirect lighting.
If she could have come again this year
she'd have had Yorkshire pudding with the roast beef
because it's Christmas. The dining room is a quarter full.
The same quiet people. Waiters in black and white;
at each place, little paper cups
filled with candied Jordan almonds in white and pink.

Later tonight, there will be church,
another tangible dock to visit dazzled and amused
like a tour of a marshland as we become exotic birds,
wade in the shallows, boasting of our crocodiles.
We will hold candles and hug strangers.

After church, a fire of fir and madrone,
we open the presents that have lain
beside the black Japanese chest in the living room.

And with the bill, a last paper cup arrives
this time with salted walnuts which sometimes
she eats and sometimes she saves for later.

Brunch at the Don César

Almost a funeral cortege we parade your gleaming
causeways, take glass elevators to the giddy
Jell-O-colored plaza of anybody's pink deco hotel.

Sun glitters the sea. Beefy bellmen tote old guests
in their wheelchairs down the grand marble stairs
as the ancients twitter like fearful birds brooding.

In the men's room next to the stack of monogrammed
towels Mick Jagger softly sings *Sympathy for the Devil*.
Leave him a dollar on the white plate and continue

roaming rooms of floral-clad women with immense
sunglasses and Fellini hats like straw dirigibles. Nearby
polo-shirted men brunch with patent leather belts.

Salt and fruity cocktails perfume the conditioned air.
The same old pusses from childhood, their retirements
spent in the funeral home on Fourth Street in St. Petes.

At each table a patriarch reigns with his leather purse,
on every plate a rose-colored hibiscus loiters
beside hollandaise or crème fraîche with mint. Again

I milk my family to give you suck. Florida, my favorite
victim, sprawled there between the sea and gulf, I hated
you on sight. Where is my Winter? Where is my Fall?

Our tanned and gilded wallet, my cousin, silver-haired,
Cadillac-cocooned, is our old moon. Long past now
when his daughter's ripe rump gigged my jaded glance.

Thick bacon, fresh peaches layered with vague violins
always seeming to come from the next dining room,
where the flaming waiter sears your scampi on a trolley.

The ceilings flicker with the sun careening into rooms,
reflected from ponds and pools, some sea you forgot
the name of just now, the third martini sinking in.

Marshall Fields

There is the parking lot, the ruined asphalt
flowing away in the slant October sun.

There is the maid, her maroon polyester uniform.
She's in tears, this woman, trundling the dead

laundry of others past me as I walk to breakfast.
She has come to mint my pillow. The night hunt,

the wait for others who will not save her.
The hindrance, the glancing blow of dawn.

My mother did not cry. My work is to carry
what is left of her in a box in the attic.

I have told you before of the traghetti in Venice,
back and forth they go across the Grand Canal

carrying who there is to float across the void.
One euro, the passengers stand like mourners.

I carry what I can. The invasiveness of her leaving,
the low sun, this old hotel, its half-lit sign,

telling us we were expected here before.
The green tin of Frango Mints holds her all.

On the drive yesterday one field is stubble,
the next the hard char from the burning.

Perhaps I shall throw her in the river. Attended
by a little divertimento by Poulenc played on the piano.

Sanibel

I told you how the bridge changed everything.
It must have been in the sixties
when there was money to burn.
Moon shots and the like.
It brought a different class of people.
Northerners and people with money.
Cars were peaking huge,
beasts beavering down the interstate
on all that new Federal concrete.
The ferry was eventually sold to Mexico,
where I'd bet it's still in service.
We never went after the bridge was built.
We lived elsewhere.
Thought about different buildings,
stone now, not the white painted board,
watermelon on the back porch.
Sea shells and shoes on the front porch.
Rusted and bowed screen doors.
Shutters akimbo.

He that We Take

I thought, café hungry,
the wet streets rolling like bells in the rain.
Two hours till dawn, the freighter arrives
rusted from a distant port, some ex who or what,
some Gordon Liddy, some dust bin.
Hello. My father was once the boy I am before you,
over bounding and sedentary, scurrying giddy.

Willing only to be what can be remembered jagged
from sleep's apothecary. Cargo complicates.
Rain has washed the harvest grit,
the urine stains, the whole stink
and stick of summer off the land.
In the garden the chrome yellow and scarlet
zinnias have fallen to mold and sodden earth.
October proceeds about its business.
Our parents are still dead.
For dinner perhaps a piece of lamb,
curried, served with the ancient crystalized sultanas,
coarse chopped cashews and some chutney
from the tall clear bottle that looks a little
like the Westerkerk in Amsterdam
if you use your imagination
as my father always recommended.

Paper Boat

I think I can feel my brain this morning
starting to motor along on caffeine and pot.
It's trying to remember the path to eyes,
which lever controls open or shut.
Another decision. I hate the tedium of them.
Once in daylight, a wisp of something egregious.
Give me a pencil, I'll draw you a plan,
sketch some shelves to build
so every atlas knows home.
There is an emerald in the tea leaves
but imagine some hasty times in Bangor,
this evening everyone is in the pub.
A de Kooning nude hangs over the bar.
I have great confidence that Spring will come again.
Climb out of darkness with the rest of us.
I'm often wrong; wrong check out line,
wrong day to shop for shoes and parsnips.
I hear my father there in the other room,
shuffling his cards all to decorate me,
put a paper hat on my head,
place me in the pond,
see if the wind will move me along.

Wanted

Someone glossy,
someone ready to explain the mirage.
My father in heaven is laughing.
He said there is a glimmer and I should tell you about it.
Please, call me direct, collect.
I am clean mostly and a good listener.
The scriptures and pronouncements of the oracle
have been distilled from wild roses.
Please include a photograph of your mother.
She is to have low miles and be candy apple red.
A personality is a plus.
Please smile into the phone if you call.
If a man answers call back on Thursday.
It is the day before the crucifixion.
Bring some cherries or other fresh fruit.
The price is negotiable.
I am waiting.

Family Gathering

That bitch of a sister will be there
and what's his name,
the one who was dropped as a baby.
Hello, I say aging rapidly,
My name is Bonehead, Hello. My name is Tulip.
The children when they can are usually more than noise,
so we need to leave before they pop the balloons.
My teeth glisten at every camera.
Please sir may I have alcohol?
Fuck the linen napkins, we sit
in the shade of the garage on white plastic chairs.
Laura is a bit slow for fifteen,
but big.
All her uncles like the thin dresses she wears.
Hello, I say
My name is Wendell Willkie
and I am the President of the United States.
Please kiss my ear.
One of my great aunts is a bell tower.
She rings her own ocean.
It is about tides.
Hello, I hear my tongue again.
Mother is always dead or smiling at these affairs.
Hello, I say, *Are you my father?*
Someone has run off with the yella' cake.
I was fixin' to have a thick moist slice.
My teeth continue glistening.

Old Boxes

My brother is in the house of the Lord,
or so my mother would say. We never
talked about the death, but she was fond
of saying, *Willie would be 28 today if he had lived.*

At the time I didn't know what to say to that.
Still don't. I used to think there was something
wrong with me to not feel more for this unmet child,
my senior silent partner, today, sitting in my small

cardboard city of boxes, finding his death certificate.
He would be 72. Some stranger, some bit of lamp light.
I feel tattered, no messages on the answering machine.
The last of the dogwood leaves should fall today.

Monday Afternoon

In a room across the world
my wife plays the piano.
The birch across the lane
has lost almost all its leaves.

The individual notes glimmer
like the landscapes of Klimpt.
Later she will walk
with an old love in the rain.

November holds its cards close.
Wait awhile, contradict,
worry, the sky French gray,
I shall go and rake some leaves.

Square

Tuesday I stopped by Goodwill with bags of clothes, scarves, odds and ends of my old life. The last thing I dropped into their blue plastic bin was the carpenter square I used to build that house you and I owned when we were we. With the old square gone I imagine the walls are now free to slump out of plumb. The floors may give up their struggle with gravity, losing their hold on level. The joints, where beam meets column, let go a little like my ancient shoulders. Each day verticality seems more abstract. Up becomes farther away; the pull of the earth less gentle.

How do you define yourself?

To begin I am a toaster,
not the toast,
a reader not the red and read,
analog anthracite.
I sit in grapefruit trees,
swim in the green lake water.
I am a boat, so are you.
I take eggs over easy.
I am endless, repeating,
obedient to geometry.
I am an equal and an opposite.
I am never cinnabar, but
I am here to box your compass.
Let's walk down to Amnesia
on the Herengracht for a toke.
I'll show you the scars,
point out the missing teeth.
I never trusted ventriloquists
and you'd be wise not to either.

Bernard Buffet 1957

The last of birch and larch leaves
have blown down on Thanksgiving,
opening again the winter vistas.
One can see through the firs a mile distant,
where my avenue loses itself in the city.
Here is where I will love you.
I am your newspaper dancing down the street.
Le Monde read at a back table in the café
where the fancies go to age.
Nunca, sing the voices from old tangos.
With this weather there will be ice
on the Canal St. Denis by Christmas.
Tempered with a cognac and a glass of mother's milk,
each morning is the fishhook
some god has given us to feed the day.

Winters ago photographing the Pont Dieu;
Buffet's painting of the same bridge
becomes the instrument by which you are called.
Hello, I'll be the bridge,
the metal arch rusting beneath your feet.

As the body drops away I suppose
the organs shrivel until at the point of death
they are but a cluster of raisins
hung in the starched and empty cathedral.
My mother's body would sing like a gourd.

Further Travel Adventures

Somewhere the boarding pass, beltless trousers, blue serge and the walleyed pike; this with her mouth full of beets before the saucy looks the rain gave us. Behind us the man, who lives in the apartment below the one in which Hemingway lived in 1928, keeps repeating, *No catheter please.* Later we go for croissants.

Traveling through the Dark

The stewardesses have stopped serving wine.
The people who can stand them
watch the tiny pale screens
where several John Travolta movies are offered.
Somewhere below, the bars in Reykjavik
are closing or not closing.
Next time I'll bring sleeping pills.
I'll bring relaxation tapes.
Next time, I'll take a boat,
I'll lobby congress for a rail line to Siberia,
anything to get me off this plane.
Give me a baguette, a glass of wine in a café
with a little sun canting in a side window,
before I push myself over the edge.

The Old Woman in the Yellow House

Here a sputum of oddments to underscore
this descent. Today the rain is but a mist,
a remembrance of last night. She's
still smoking because
she's focused on the tragic death.
How the lungs putrefy.
No wind.
The old pause to deal with the momentary,
the shudders and farts. He cinches up his belt
an extra notch, blue serge. Near the old folks'
home is a private park where the ancients
go to sit by the river amid the goose shit —
to understand about loneliness,
how the earth must feel, infested
with organisms with the morals of a virus;
the nearest others constrained by gravity
to different paths.

What Night Said

When I was in the Blue building at the Portland zoo
murky water in the penguin compound convinced me,

don't make it a felony, to give someone a reason
to break up with poetry, feel the beefy paw of prose

on one's shoulder. For the obvious reasons, the slick,
the reek of fish — not trout almandine either,

just rank and nasty vats of guts. I'd rather have deep
fried walleye pike stuffed with Canadian bacon.

This isn't a poem. I don't know, maybe the little beasts
like the stuff. A bit of entrail when the noon whistle

gets the juices flowing. My friends in America send me
ideas for poems, but here in the blue morning hours

by a French river, all the same fears. The night dogs
barking, the saliva, their thick and heady smell.

Not the penguins from Sam or carnations and brass
buttons Joy sent. Please, take them away.

Penguins, why penguins? I haven't been to a zoo
in years. It was never about fish, it was always the bars.

Belgium, canned corn,

mascara. Trying to find the trail, the small accolades and blood stains, tweezers. There is an anteater at the zoo in Antwerp, Belgium. I don't know how long they live, that one must be dead by now. It was that long ago, a nail clipper with a Canadian flag. There was a trace, a track. Some Boy Scout with an axe led the way. In Belgium corn is considered an animal feed in the caramelized-onion crowd. a white plastic bottle of Oxycodone. The old starry geography of empires become trams of tourists in big white shoes and gaudy summer colors, lemon yellow, French blue, a hemostat. I hadn't intended to go to Antwerp, but I took the wrong train. Small sips of coffee make it last. *Hello, You have exceeded the baggage allowance of one garment, one sack of ash – the rest is to be left behind.* In one tank in the darkened room a moray eel waits. I'd recommend the beer, a frayed wash cloth, a pair of small scissors, a tube of ointment.

Book Tour

And so the famous poet moves on across the land
selling his sparklers and bottle rockets.
Don't try this at home, he says adjusting his poet hat.
For a wink and a caramel and $28.95
he'll sign the damn chicken you're strangling.

Venice

The peppermint girls are back.
The red tutus, white stockings, the saucy looks.
We should be wrapping things up here
on the brink of desire.

After the fire the days are sodden, smoky air.
Polish the bronze bier we use to tote the failures.
Here's one holding out his hand
for a last touch of the world.

I don't know which train we travel on.
Check the metal placards on each platform.
One says, *mother*, another, *death*.
Do not return through these portals.

If you think I'm making this up,
look in the mirror. Write your name on the rock.
Later we build a different Stonehenge
or something else heavy.

Swordfish lurk on the luggage rack above,
bathed in the vermillion platitudes of this new order,
we have a Coke for twenty euros
under the purple bougainvillea.

The music was too loud in the photo. We hook
our safety lines, sought what we seldom found.
She poses in Venice, 22, sitting on a white marble sill,
her rapacious casement. The world spilt out.

Mother is waiting with shamans and priests,
and our birthrights bought at the Thursday market.
The boys at the fish stall wait, white aprons
impermeable with desire.

The woman turned to me, her mouth full
of beets. The red juice like blood on her blouse.
Windows open, we serenade the town.
The volume burns our ears.

Getting from Amsterdam to Paris

Monday, my arm hurts. Something small chews.
The black beyond the pain, some dawn close now.
Outside, moving, moaning rain and train horns.
It's going to be today all day with cone collars
to amuse. And unseemly and gorgeous words
for how we squirm. My torn shoulder amuses me,
my best god and swinging door.
Beat down grasses.
Waiting for the bus he kept talking
to his cell phone, *Blah, blah,*
a urinary tract infection.
The cows are watching us watch them.
Particles accrue. It's going to be Monday
all day with Mercury too close to the sun to see,
at least for most of us lovelies on the bus.
The surface tension was an honorable skirmish.
layered like sheep waiting for that same bus.
He was drawing the same figure again, again.
Stooped, overcoated like an old man.
Walking toward you an old woman
bent under shopping bags, or a boy, say his body
draped in bombs. *Hello, it's Monday.*
The settings are always different.
Empty shoe horn, without you.
Beside the river somewhere between Paris
and where the light runs out
there is a road, a path really,
two tire ruts in a wheat field. Follow me.

Beside the Lake

> Though I am frail here in my bunting
> Taliesin

Mother said,
The pregnant woman in 9C is being a problem,
but I was the only one in that ward.

I am croaking over and over,
No catheter please. He reaches
for the covers, sanitizes white enamel stanchions.

The tight wakes of skywriters arc above
tell us of secret words
kissed by the dead, claiming to be ancestors

no one recalls them or the small gods
that made us, each curve,
each splendid wart. To say senseless days

are almost gone is optimistic. They await only
someone from the Times with a camera;
meanwhile a beefy doctor is bending over the bed.

The River Vézère

Her clothes are a picnic lunch, heavy with mangos,
peaches and other such supplicants with their thick

moist flesh. This was days later, hours before
her death at the rented house where the river

forced its banks each May. In St Petersburg
at the bookstore across from St Paul's he bought

a copy of *The Waste Land*. It brought back the
remembrance of the taste of the pale fig jam

she served when we stopped last year. In the garden
they drank wine as they turned over the earth

with spading forks, their fingers sticky with the tokay.
Still no one is looking at the boy,

no one asking, no one is speaking those thick old
Hungarian words that take them back to Budapest.

The vines are cranking round, looking for the sun
while the big blue Skoda tractor works the rows.

At night the calls creep in on shafts of darkness.
She will be there to follow the trail we left in crumbs,

our history the last track back to the beginning.
I would have waited for you, but I never got the call.

Portugal

Warm rags,
riding side-saddle again.
The sign says,
This is the beginning again.
I wrote the sign,
a side line of mine. It is because
of fine lines, philosophies, dandruff shampoos.
Tomorrow we will go dance in the old
second floor ball room with the creaky floor.
I will dance with Toni.
So bold this morning to predict the future —
other women park their horse carts on the byways.
Death tends to undo beginnings. I gave up
on pajamas when I left home.

Old streetcars in Lisbon are repainted for tourists from far Manhattan.

Nude is a way of holding the body, open as a door, a fuse. The local nudists have a camp north of the river. They are old and tan, self-desiccating jockeys; their horses asleep by the pool. My naked is the boy, the sparrow, the oaks in November. Burghers, old meat met once too many. They grind around the city's steel loops.
Naked opens.
There are sparks falling from above.
Receiving life as cleanly as the lily does the bee.

Turkey

My dinner with the roast squab was better
than the dinner we got
out of the machine at the airport.
It was better than anything
the other boy scouts ate
at the camp out on Jefferson Key.
The fish is held up above the tank for approval.
The hungry man nods,
the other asks the price.
Fish is expensive in Kushadasa,
but worth the price.
The same dinner at home couldn't be found.
This isn't Peoria, said the fish.
I continue to be disoriented.
Kushadasa was a long time ago.
Everyone else who was there
has gone on with their lives.

The Montana Caucus

Waking to snow, the shocking absence
of socialist thugs now when we need them the most.
Acquiescence tasting of zinc. *Red Chalk*, the Indian said,
Let's go to Amsterdam for a blowjob and a tasty-freeze.

The grease champion, an old man
with a week's white whiskers and a fish eye fumbles
for a tobacco and papers. He's you or me
back when we smoked in the old days,
checked into the Hotel Quincy
with a pseudonym for sex.

On the morning news another wonder dog
has rescued the blind cheerleader from the well.
Thank God, we think,
going about our oatmeal and Spanish verbs.
In far Idaho the elaborate are buried, caramelized.

We sometimes and sometimes not. *You follow me?* I am
saying, *Hello. It's another day, time to put on our shoes.* The
dwarf in the wheel chair is coming for pinochle. I want
to surprise him with a homemade prune Danish.

The Upper Peninsula of Michigan

My sister Alice is my favorite person.
Before dawn the utter stillness
of the lake focuses me.
We're very alike and unlike.
She eats soup with a small spoon.
Oarlocks in place.
I, a large spoon.
She has the face of our mother,
the Madonna.

Padding out onto the dock.
In the boat gentle to not wake the lake.
Loosen the night,
and pull away,
weaving a chain of angels in clear water.

Later I shall make tea,
carry it to her in the other room,
rub her temples, draw her a bath to row across.

Amsterdam

I like those
cows, she said,
looking
at the black and white lithograph on the kitchen wall.

Earlier, we had bought milk this morning at Jumbo's.
Three cows, placid, lying in a neutral background.
Sunday morning, all cigarette butts and bicycles
chained to black iron railings.
Beside the coolers,
holding two cold cartons in my hands.
But when
she moved on in her conversation,
began speaking about engaging the Dutch magnetron,
I forgot, and had to ask again
what she had said about cows.

Biloxi Morning

A thick and sullen beating of wings, the Palmetto bug
clambers for position in the dark wooden shutters.

I can make out its shadows in the predawn.
Little broken pieces of its dark fussing,
there in silhouette.

When you get back with the beer we will sit outside
on the porch and watch the sun come up.

This Week

Monday

Get the woman in the yellow dress to tell you
about the fire. What went wrong.
Flames licking at the ceiling.
The wallpaper ablaze.

Pastoral scenes of the chateau at Cherbourg
disappearing in the smoke.
The sun springs up,
hands us another day to root for tubers.

The listeners are deaf and the orators dumb,
but out on the boulevard
another day delivers the pancakes and asphalt.
We argue zoning issues.
She is looking at her glass of wine
as if preparing a comment
on the color, its oakiness, its smooth finish.
But I think she is remembering Tuscany,
or some place where things happened
because of the wine.

Some day the water will be calm enough
for the ferries to resume service.
The traffic on the avenue,
each barge or boat or barque that sails
downstream passes by my toll booth,
pays me in images of chromium and coquinas
Look at that, I say. We move closer.

Everyone waiting is polite,
knowing those at the front of the line
may be receiving unpleasant surprises
even as we speak.

Tuesday

My hearing is beginning to go,
old men lean forward in noisy restaurants.
I rot, hold printouts of blood tests, bone scans.

Here is a long list of women who are no longer of
interest to me. Whose tight white slacks
are released to walk up other streets.

This was the gist of the conversation:
old guys bitching, licking
their wounds with thick tongues,
prunes for the bowels. Outside

fruit ripens: *Sophisticates*, say the scientists.
Plums fall with no sound.
Quince hang in trees waiting for us
to develop a taste for bitterness.

Wednesday

My teeth were on fire again this morning when I awoke.
I could lay on the tracks, pretend to be Grand Rapids
and suicidal.

There is too much shrubbery.
Am I going too fast for you?
We knew it would be difficult after the fall of Nixon.
And later

we had drinks on what passes for Route 66 today.
Which is to say something past, going before, something
with the juice wrung out.

Thursday

Two taverns and the drunk
can't make up his mind. Outside
workers scarved against the chill
gleam in the persimmon light.

Each morning just past dawn
I rise to look out my window,
see the work of night complete,
almost the same people,

almost the same autos and snapdragons.
Weedy yards becoming
the gold of harvest moons,

but still we piss our boots, the war goes on,
when all we want is a world
where everyone's dog has a bone.

Friday

The bedroom we shared was round. We made Lydia
sleep in the trailer because of the power of her snoring.

Each day the sun comes up like a bad penny
to coin a phrase.
So we are in the bedroom.
The woman is saying, *never*

and *right now* which I take as confusing.
What your god is always asking us to do.
The pope will let us know.

He sets and arcs the basketball for a swisher.
Papal infallibility,
she says to me with a wink.
Martyrs stand around our bed.

Pascal tapers blazing. In the corner
a great pile of discarded vestments.
Purples, gold brocades, stoles, albs and cassocks.

We'll take it all to Goodwill.
Soon wild-eyed street people
with be celebrating mass on each corner.

Cardboard signs saying, *This is my body. Take. Eat,*
Do this in remembrance of me.

Saturday

Something will be different today,
will make me stop and raise
my head, check for the scent of musk in the long grass.

Something will be new today,
some glint becomes a star, an errant
moon, some fresh gravity to bend our lights,
refresh the spectrum's laze.

Something in the garden will bloom or ripen
as you do daily. Born also only for the hours
we hold as the coins in this economy of two.

Sunday

The traffic on the boulevard is thin today.
So I can hear the fly, the clock,
the neighborhood hunkered down
to take its leisure supine.

One might count paupers or egrets.
Hobbies fill the time. The sky its thick
and windless self. Behind the house,
last night's chairs serpentine the yard.

I am wrung of desire, slammed,
a yellow feather on the day.

Get the woman in the yellow dress
to tell you about fire. *Flames learn to climb
before they can talk*, she says.

Occasionally August

The sun reels past; the forbidden fruit piles up, some effete treats in small spaces before the last of the good watermelons. Labor Day, like a persimmon but not as orange, rounds the corner. The CIA takes out Lumumba.

Considering the End of Summer

September is still a shortage.
A brief wit exposed
at the end of a long life.
September, the voting continues late into the evening.
Shooting can be heard from the rooftops.
There is a great gauze of spider webs
forming on the spent garden.
Eurydice walks beyond the hedge. It is September.
There are six bottles of water in the garage.
Only six bottles.
The results of the election are blue green, aqua to teal.
September is still months away,
thick ankled and up hill.
Threadbare August is our last vanguard.
This Eurydice doesn't believe, asks for a transfer.
It's September,
the few on the boat deck still have on summer attire.
My father has been gone twenty years,
but for the face I shave each morning.
September is as it does, wakes to the distant klaxon.
The last good watermelon. Labor Day.
Welcome home vets.
We swat flies. Each day the apples weigh more.
With you September would be
the chestnuts beside the Café Renard.
Here where June slips into July, a lover lingering.
Hold out.
Be kind if you can.
The tomatoes are coming.

Port Townsend in Rain

The old folks are out on the bluff waiting for the dog
to bark again. The famous poet is bitching. Someone
erased her poem as if it were a mere de Kooning.

The famous former director wears corduroy
to tantalize the new boys. You understand
we, the misfits, have been waiting a long time.

It's called a peninsula, said the guide, *like persimmon,
but not as orange.* Wheelbarrows have been piling up
beside the parade ground for years.

What is this shit? says someone in the front row
where the visiting car salesmen sit. The driver
of the truck that hauls away the shit wears white.

Every morning the same language lurks in my mouth.
It's Christmas 1940, France has fallen. Bending
her back on the small mahogany bed he enters her.

Presents for everyone, Michael. The obligations
of a just god are kindness and good planning,
perhaps this explains each tornado ours sends us

with tinsel and a bone-colored card engraved *God*
in a dainty typeface. *Best Wishes*, scrawled
across its face in her snotty green ink.

It's the age, said the poet with the precious poet hat.
Cooking is a habit I pick up from the gypsies.
They stole my grandmother once —

least that's the story getting passed around
in the tea leaves. The beers keep coming.
The famous poets are pierced by fire.

Dancers

The dancers were standing out back of Jordan's Bar,
smoking and fiddling with their eyelashes.

Reverend Ted didn't look, he smelled their smoke.
Nine years ago Buffy, the big redhead,

had been in his first confirmation class at St Bart's.
Then her name had been Laurie Mae.

Ted carries a Pall Mall in his pocket. Only one,
carefully wrapped with a kitchen match

in a sarcophagus folded from a three by five card,
a little life boat should the weather deteriorate.

He quit three weeks ago, but kept that cigarette`
for religious reasons. *Forbidden fruit*, he thinks.

Curious

You might be thinking about her again.
The way she could stand still as ice.

Just now in the heat, the sun reeling past,
the days have an ancient bake.
How might you think of friendship?
Two barefoot boys some place
like this, August warm.
You might remember anything
from those days,
the canal, the bikes abandoned like dead horses?
So few faces anymore,
you might remember
the red haired girl we were in love with.

Just Then

Excepting cellophane-wrapped cookies from the lobby,
he hadn't had an Oreo in two years. Remember, no
rules. The minute that escaped was yesterday.

Xavier Cugat was a natty dresser, flagrantly self-aware.
He taught white America beginnings, the rumba,
the use of the cloth hand towel, effete treats in small
spaces.

In the middle of that strange century, the barking dog.
My gmail sidebar is all ads for surgery and pain killers.
1961, 1935, the CIA takes out Lumumba.

No rules. Somewhere between then and *forever*.
The doc said he won't prescribe pain medication
because it would eventually lose efficacy.

The wind is blowing the dress against her, outlining
her body against pale cerulean, the clothes line.
Towels roughened in the wind in a place without walls.

We hope our birthrights keep the balloons up forever.
We have not yet talked about the toads, you and I.
Wonderful beasts, but they are prone to pissing if held,

old diesel, chum, etcetera. Kay says, there was
champagne when the balloon landed.
It's a nasty new dance we call the samba.

Thursday

Take away the knife. Which small opera shall we sing?
I am not a voice you will hear again. In the heat we bray,
donkeys challenging dawn, those who make our soup.

The way we live is by the cook. Celery and a bit of beef.
Watch the moon walk the water. We salvaged
a few small prayers. Listen again. The waters cleanse.

We are broke. Breathe in morning's scent,
the silver girls waiting in the surf. Sirens,
wish a new zephyr to purify us. The sun a grapefruit,

the sky all raisins and wishes. Refuse what you will.
I remember days like cherries. Animate the clock.
Please be the meeting of azure sky, cobalt sea.

Storms move off over the mountains beyond the olive
groves and narrow doorways. Byways, each cough,
each cigarette. Now rotating round the planet

by degrees, Cancer and Capricorn in a wheat field.
Wind caresses the heavy heads. August
lays wooly on the land. *Father,* we say, *Forgive us.*

Grant again the gift of fire. Here is my heart, unleavened.

Give each snake its rage, its due. At Cana Christ gave
wedding goers wine. It is grace, this remembrance,
the unwished gift. The silver arrow of time pricks us.

The girls in the bar must wonder where we are.
The bear is the sky, last slip of soap, heel of bread.
What was sought is what we left behind.

She said, *Wednesday*, but I knew Thursday was the day
Christ and the disciples shared tangerines and apples,
plus plums, sweet meats and the jugs of red, red wine.

It's a party. Now really, don't take this the wrong way,
but this train can only follow the tracks laid down
by others. In our breasts the remains of what we own.

In our magneto hearts each sun is set, each cloud born.
I have come back. I wander only in the dream of you.
The woman is this girl I love, but never Wednesday.

Dead at 98º

Cauterized and zinc-like the odor of a room where meat
had been hung. *My time is coming,* the guard said to me. I
said, *Don't worry. The pain is a reminder.*

Facts are birch leaves scattered across November yet
each morning reflects my father's face in the mirror.
Down at the end of the dial they're showing old movies.

Some get used to the food, come to expect it after awhile.
Jeff Chandler and Victor Mature argue in the game
room. We take the oatmeal with two sugars.

Should I go back to school at my age? Study
the 21st century American novel or syphilis among
French whoremongers during the second empire?

The old man in the chair turned 110 two days back.
He enjoys the warmth. I told him not to worry.
We'll borrow some sugar from another table.

the Gabor sisters take their leave

Because now, near the end, everything winds down to a level of background radiation that some of us, even Ted, have learned to tolerate. We are beyond the Schengen controls, the horizon already speckled with our lush debris, nearby armadillos huddle expectantly.

Blondie

With her stiletto heels dawn arrives again,
her arms grappling with the sky,
it's the usual boring dark mumblings,
talk of disrespect.
She has the muffins of rain in a paper sack,
but the honey is left over from the wars
of the last century. They are recognizable
from their odor of sobriety, but are sticky.
Meanwhile we continue to wait in line,
the voice that called assures us
there will still be enough daylight
if we can just hold on long enough
to find the artificial horizon
on the instrument panel. Tomorrow we
begin the journey back to the interior.
Head home where January or high summer waits.
Offload the obscene print of Egon Schiele
plus other trinkets of less intimacy.
All we purchased with hard currency
waits now by the sallyport on the Lido deck.
You remember,
someone always seems on the verge of dancing.
The woman in the red dress has taken
her skinny ass back to Ypsilanti.
Picasso is still telling fortunes. The rest of us
will get on with sunset. Each day
we grow shorter, closer to the earth.

Early October

The boat is hung from the boathouse rafters.
The green tomatoes are wrapped in newspaper,
hosta and agapanthus cut back to the ground.
The dog knows, and the cat too.
The geese are low over the house,
the sun too. On the lawn now
the morning dew hangs till three.
I stand in the back yard
rake in hand watching the maple leaves
still clutching their branches in foolish hope.

Yesterday afternoon

when we walked back from the bibliothèque
where we go to use the internet, two swans
were feeding in the diminished Vézère.

October has drawn down the water from the vernal
floods that covered the quays, so now
one could wade across.

My wife is practicing her French. She tells me
of the *petit oiseau*, that sang so sweetly
in the pre-dawn cold.

She discusses with our neighbor the best place to park
our *voiture*, which day to put out the yellow
sack of recycling or the black *poubelle*.

She sits now *au soleil* eating the last croissant
from the buttery bag. She adds no butter
to the flaky crust. Only the red jam

of strawberries and raspberries from the Intermarché
across the river. A dollop escapes her knife,
falls blood red on the white tile.

Small Camera

All the possums had names
with the same number of syllables.
They carried this burden as best they could.
At a distance, say across the big bog, their names
became only familiar lumps of sound.

Lime trees lined the boulevard as far as the rail crossing.
They reminded him of Berlin,
a place he had never been.

Quill is the magenta you hear at dusk.
Hello again, I keep missing you at the bus stop.
I didn't see you in Paris,
at the dumpster behind Hoot's
where we take our *déjeuner*.
May I recommend the blue plate special?
Yes?
No?
He peers out of the family photograph
from the nineteenth century.

Quill is the boy who taught us to whistle in the dark.
All along Battery Park, chestnuts litter the ground.
It's late October, all winter Quill will leave the shades up
to bring in enough light to make it through the day.

Try again, here, see if this helps,
he was leaning over, holding
something out that festooned down Quill's body.

You're not sure the tightness
in the chest is the tightening
they speak of with alarm.
It could have been
the chicken on white,

you could have asked
for extra mayo to slide it home.
Delusion is the penny
we pay to look into the mirror.
Their flagellations are bereft of wit and charm.
The first to go followed the traces of the dancers
who of course left town long ago,
seeking a piper, any piper.
It shows only who has moved on
in their private affairs, and who not.
Where he disappeared was sleek.
It was a place of sacrifice,

it was a place smelling of ozone,
machine oil and milk.
It reminded him of mother,
of the notch and slam of growing.

There's always Veronica Lake against
some buttress, some lamp post, some
pickup truck. *Honey, Honey,* says the jukebox.
Some days are a leaky pen and a bald tire.
But some nights live behind the curvature
of the earth, happenstance, the hocus pocus
of the hour. A spare tire once occupied
the well in the trunk. Alas no more.
Quill is thinking, I was hornswoggled.
But he can hear them calling for more
possum in the dining room, so, drying
his hands on the long white apron, he pushes
through the door to the dining room
just like in the Fellini movie.

My White-Hot Mirror Has Cheek at Night

Literal and lateral and detonation and.
You are too literal, the stencil read.
I never wanted anything like he, she, it, us,
the box waiting outside the door.
I ordered it. She sent it. It was a gift.
It was immense.
I never wanted anything so crumpled, so white boy,
so turnip and palm fronds.
I never wanted the hiatus, hiccup, halitosis.
I'll be the mongrel in the box, never wanting.
I'll be immense in the box outside the door
which you are on the other side of
wanting and not wanting
and doing everything just right
to be immense and perfectly you, crumpled.
As if our epoch passed fast enough
that we could etch its arc across the sky.

My mother was frank not long-winded.
Don't talk to them, she said.

It's about plate tectonics, global warming
or some errant chunk of space debris.
Some voyager from the dark out beyond Neptune
to come traipsing our way.

We live in the resident creation,
house, castle, hovel, home.
Hello, I say at the door with a grin.
Later I imagine what went first.
Who pushed the big green START button.
In being I always find old Sartre
spinning his theories like a fishmonger in heaven.
There is the hum of heavy industry, the engine room,
or the generator hall of some great dam.

The whole of the earth wants to sing.
Gratefully to find help, not some hooligan
come to break each resident with their own bones
or deliver them to what small ice flows may remain.

Leaving their minds in search of castle, hovel, home.
Hold the battery terminals,
hoping for soda and ash.
So I answer the phone less eagerly than before.
It seems to be about growing smaller.
Walking some gravel road back to childhood,
hoping one hook is still empty
to hang my hat on in that musty cloak room.

New Book

Black and white photos of the old ball rooms. Giddy
colors gone gray. Gauzy gowns flounced. Jade green

chiffon fades, the Gabor sisters take their leave.
Someone was drunk on the other side of the wall.

Thursday after the alcoholics leave, oldsters dance
in the church basement under the paper stars.

Too much to drink, everyone will frolic with Korean
businessmen here to study urea-based fertilizers.

Tomorrow the ritual stoning of Dick Cheney will again
be reenacted to satisfy the peoples' need for blood.

Night chills, remembering — window still open —
the cold. The yellow gleam of a distant neighbor

remote as a star, no sound from the road. Shivered
thinking about the $4,000. It must do. If she got up

she would freeze on the spot. When finally the alarm
sounds the badgers will bring coffee and croissant.

They would shut the window, bring her an afghan
from the sunroom. The clock struck three. Crap!

The badgers wouldn't be here for three more hours.
It was the first snowfall. Remember the quiet?

The streets are French Impressionist, Doctor Zhivago.
The citizens with feet bundled soundless against cold.

Outside the snow paused and a few tardy flakes
settled to melt immediately on the pavement.

No Russian Christmas this year. No sledding,
No turkey galantine and champagne flutes at midnight.

He'd never noticed the door let into the wainscoting
in a most cunning way to disguise its existence.

Never noticed the way she sat, looking at the door
as if clouds were drifting past and today was a summer

like the ones father had spoken of before the war.
The banners for that war still hanging in the rafters.

Live life in small nuggets, fragments, unaware time
slips away, sitting by the river watching the flow,

the eddies so apparently innocent, random and placid
as the river curls its way on down to the sea.

Santorini, Crete or Corniglia

At the kitchen table we would sit for days eating toast. In the distance, thunder of a new war coming to the neighborhood with its tubas, flutes and bazookas. Too much sun leading to some fresh brain fever creeping up from Africa. Of the gasoline we knew nothing.

At the kitchen table the toaster is red hot and weary of the monotony of a steady job. Our day we hear only the distant thunder of others out saving the world one postage stamp at a time. Too much sun is pouring in the windows of our little breakfast room, so we squint at the morning prunes and paper asking them questions which we have no right to know.

At the kitchen table morning is already half through its busy day of cutting silhouettes for old Sol to paper our whitewashed walls. Too much sun already radiates the white town stair-stepping down to the sea, cerulean and cold. The distance, the thunder that is the horse hour, dawn, has left us used, savaged. The moment she chooses for arrival underscores her descent, fall, her loss of reason.

At the kitchen table, the broken yokes flood toast like daffodils in spring, careless. That distant thunder is the last raw thing making its exit or some new spectacle for the bowed and broken. Just now they come exhausted by life creeping up and down the aisles of Winco dressed in muumuus, pajama bottoms and flip flops. How very Maury and Jerry and Geraldo of them aping our imagination. Here are the dog walkers of Buenos Aires, their packs of dogs all wearing the same collar. The same name on each collar. When they found him they bowed down.

At the kitchen table, speckled now with our lush debris, the scent of bacon still lingering like the remembrance of the woman in a dress the color of garnets. I digress now and could conjure up a love poem all blamed on too much sun. That distant thunder comes still with its penchant for both showmanship and banality, the ability to brush off the remainders like a valet at his master's side. Tell me this, is it my imagination? He is the one who glitters? Sending off showers of sparks when irritated?

But at our kitchen table the dishes have been cleared. The sun has moved on, a slave to duties in the western realm, some armadillos to warm, an ice cap to melt. Distant thunder, lightning and rain have moved on leaving the streets wet and clean; ready for whatever heap man serves up next.

Indecision

My father thought Unitarians believed too little and Catholics believed too much. I don't know. He was good as he was able, but I am only good when the wind is with me. It's a symphony for the deaf, this life. I stoop to grasp the shiny stones. If I were an eagle or a cat we would not be talking thus — of loneliness and death. Turn off the air conditioning, turn down the sound, if we walk beside rivers we become the fish. When you tell me the earth is supported by tortoises I think, *Well, that's as good a way as any*. Still, I don't know. Outside February snow mixes with rain. Today is the Sabbath, and as always we will depend on the stoutness of each carapace, each caprice.

Running in the Dark
> We are like sculptors, constantly carving out
> of others the image we long for... Anais Nin

Railroad tracks parallel the beach, the brick highway.
Only fools trust roads leading home;
best trust the phases of the moon.

We are the hooligans on this Ferris wheel,
the sky filled with swans. Father, dead thirty years,
cries, *Hosanna!* No longer remembers

the names of his gods. *We are from the old testament*,
they jeer. *We are Coptic priests*,
intone these benefactors, shamans and prostitutes.

Desire waits fertile, something un-French, the Subte
to the *jardín biológico* for sauerkraut and schnapps,
An odd habit, said Madam.

We were still speaking Spanish behind her back. The
days waiting, interminable. Finally the men come
about the French woman's effects.

Porcelain doll heads hand made in Dresden
before the RAF excised it from the map.
A signed photograph of Anais Nin. So it goes.

The last image through the train window: the priest
walking back from the cemetery. He carried
the all six volumes of Gibbon's *Decline*.

I wonder what I should have saved. I have a few
old vestments, a railroad schedule, boxes of words,
pressed roses; useless things. The building

burned all night. Someone called the *pompiers*,
but none had arrived when we started walking
back up the tracks toward town.

Acknowledgements

Thanks to my wife, Toni Hanner, for inspiration, support and endless rereadings of this collection, to Tom Aslin for his careful reading and suggestions. Most of the poems in this volume have benefited in one way or another with exposure to either Red Sofa Poets in Eugene and Madrona Writers in Port Townsend.

Biloxi Morning appeared in *Verseweavers* No. 12.
My Birthday Sonnet appeared in *Verseweavers* No.14.
Christmas Eve and *Old Boxes* appeared in *Nimrod*.
Turkey, Blondie, Yesterday Afternoon and *Conveyance* were published in *Confessions of Autumn*.
A City appeared in *Conversations Across Borders*
Sarasota, Indecision, More Geography, Turning the Boats over Each Fall, The Upper Peninsula of Michigan, Amsterdam, What Night Said and *The Old Woman in the Yellow House* were published in *The Architecture of Holland*.

What's time to a pig?

About the Author

toni hanner

Michael Hanner's poetry has appeared in *Gargoyle, Rhino, MARGIE, Nimrod, Mudfish, C.A.B., Off the Coast, Cloudbank* and many others.

Michael's chapbooks are *Closing Down the Piccolo Bar*, 2008, *Palm Sunday*, 2009, *Winter Dreams*, 2011, *The Architecture of Holland*, 2012, *Confessions of Autumn*, 2014 & *Avenida Uriburu*, 2015. His first full-length book, *Vivaldi, an autobiography*, was published in 2013. He is a member of Red Sofa and of Madrona Writers.

He worked as an architect in Chicago and later in Eugene, Oregon. He has lived in Illinois in a 19th century brick house on the Mississippi River, a shingled shack in the Florida panhandle, a cinder-block bungalow in Miami, a stone house on the north shore of Chicago, a basement apartment, a room with a linoleum floor, another bungalow with corn fields out the window, an apartment with a black-iron fire escape near the Lincoln Park Zoo, a couple of three-flats in the neighborhoods of old Lithuanians, a red farmhouse on abandoned acreage, another bungalow now in Eugene, a few houses and apartments around southwestern France, a house in a forest, a Buenos Aires one bedroom with iffy power, and now a house with a view of the avenue.

His other interests are gardening, irony, English croquet, French cooking, Argentine tango and photography. He lives in Eugene with his wife, poet Toni Hanner. He has neither a dog named named Spam, nor a cat named Mehitabel.

www.ingramcontent.com/pod-product-compliance
Lightning Source LLC
Chambersburg PA
CBHW032125090426
42743CB00007B/465